The *faith* to FORGIVE

Forgiveness Journal

JAMES MCCARROLL

Published by Holy Impact Publishing, LLC
311 Trenton Court - Murfreesboro, TN 37130

Thank you Pastor Sharon Riley for encouraging this accompanying
journal.

www.holyimpactmovement.org

To those that fueled my hope while I was learning to forgive. This is but a portion of the fruit of your sacrifice.

A Word on Forgiveness

"...For if you forgive men their trespasses, your heavenly Father will also forgive you. But if you do not forgive men their trespasses, neither will your Father forgive your trespasses." (Matthew 6:14-15)

One of the key elements to healthy fellowship with God, self and others is that of forgiveness (Luke 6:37). The word "forgive" is literally translated "to send away, to give away, to go away and leave something behind." Forgiveness is the act of dropping any emotional "charges" that come from something that is done to offend you. It is choosing to renounce your ability and right to carry out vengeance on the person that wronged you. When you choose to forgive, you choose the relationship over holding on the offense (Matthew 18:15). This opens your heart to receive love in the place of anger and resentment and positions you to be used as a vessel of the grace of God towards the offender. Also, when we ask God to forgive them, it causes a shift in our motives from hate to love and allows us to consider their best interest instead of their worst possible outcome (Colossians 3:12-14). Ultimately, forgiveness frees them from the offense and frees us from the potential poison of bitterness that comes from housing unforgiveness in our souls. It is in forgiveness that we reflect the relationship-cleansing love of the heart of God.

This accompanying journal has been designed to walk you through the process of forgiveness. Depending on the level of hurt, it may take several times of going through the process to get the wound completely resolved. I pray that as you go through this guide, your life will experience the freedom and joy that await it on the other side of releasing the offense.

PRAYER
OF FORGIVENESS

Heavenly Father, I come acknowledging the sins of my
_____(father, mother, co-worker, etc.). I know
that these sins have both direct and indirect effects on my life
and the lives of others. I pray that you would forgive them for
_____ (name the action that caused
offense). I pray that the blood of Jesus would wash this sin from
their record according to 1 John 1:9. I also pray that any curses
that are the result of this sin be sent to the cross of Christ and
not experienced by them. Finally, I forgive them for any hurt,
dysfunction, anger or damage that their actions may have caused
in my mind, heart, or body. I choose to not hold any "charges"
against them from this point forward as it pertains to this offense.
Thank you for forgiving them according to your work in Jesus Christ.

Now I confess that I have responded to their actions by
_____ (name any negative response mentally,
emotionally, physically, verbally). I ask that you would wash my sinful
response(s) in the blood of Jesus Christ. I accept your forgiveness
and ask that you would send any corresponding curses to the cross
of Jesus Christ. I rebuke any demonic forces that came into my
heart through this experience and send you from my heart. I have
been bought with a price and my life is meant to glorify God!!!!!

Now, Holy Spirit, I ask that you would fill my heart with
_____ (name the Spiritual Fruit that you
need to offset the response to the sin: love, joy, peace, patience,
faith, goodness, gentleness, self-control, meekness) so that I will no
longer respond to this action in an ungodly way, but will reflect your
heart from this moment forward. **Give the Holy Spirit a moment
to deposit the necessary spiritual fruit needed and walk in
restored health!**

Scriptures
ON FORGIVENESS

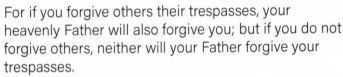

For if you forgive others their trespasses, your
heavenly Father will also forgive you; but if you do not
forgive others, neither will your Father forgive your
trespasses.
(Matthew 6:14-15)

Then Peter came and said to him, "Lord, if another
member of the church sins against me, how often
should I forgive? As many as seven times?" Jesus said
to him, "Not seven times, but, I tell you, seventy-seven
times.
(Matthew 18:22-23)

Be on your guard! If another disciple sins, you must
rebuke the offender, and if there is repentance, you
must forgive. And if the same person sins against you
seven times a day, and turns back to you seven times
and says, 'I repent,' you must forgive."
(Luke 17:3-4)

"Whenever you stand praying, forgive, if you have
anything against anyone; so that your Father in
heaven may also forgive you your trespasses."
(Mark 11:25)

SCRIPTURES
ON FORGIVENESS

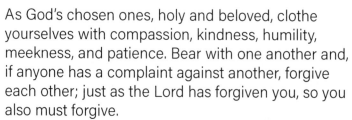

As God's chosen ones, holy and beloved, clothe yourselves with compassion, kindness, humility, meekness, and patience. Bear with one another and, if anyone has a complaint against another, forgive each other; just as the Lord has forgiven you, so you also must forgive.
(Colossians 3:12-13)

Put away from you all bitterness and wrath and anger and wrangling and slander, together with all malice, and be kind to one another, tenderhearted, forgiving one another, as God in Christ has forgiven you.
(Ephesians 4:31-32)

And forgive us our debts, as we also have forgiven our debtors.
(Matthew 6:12)

For judgment will be without mercy to anyone who has shown no mercy; mercy triumphs over judgment.
(James 2:13)

SCRIPTURES
ON FORGIVENESS

But love your enemies, do good, and lend, expecting nothing in return. Your reward will be great, and you will be children of the Most High; for he is kind to the ungrateful and the wicked. Be merciful, just as your Father is merciful.

"Do not judge, and you will not be judged; do not condemn, and you will not be condemned. Forgive, and you will be forgiven; give, and it will be given to you. A good measure, pressed down, shaken together, running over, will be put into your lap; for the measure you give will be the measure you get back."
(Luke 6:35-38)

But if anyone has caused pain, he has caused it not to me, but to some extent—not to exaggerate it—to all of you. This punishment by the majority is enough for such a person; so now instead you should forgive and console him, so that he may not be overwhelmed by excessive sorrow. So I urge you to reaffirm your love for him.
(2 Corinthians 2:5-8)

SCRIPTURES
ON FORGIVENESS

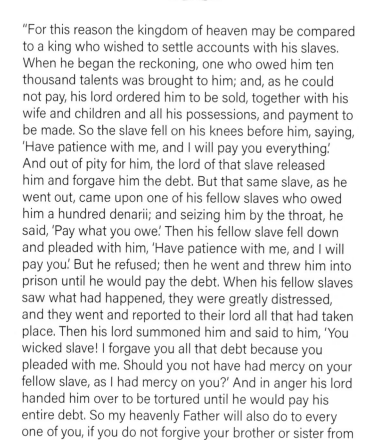

"For this reason the kingdom of heaven may be compared to a king who wished to settle accounts with his slaves. When he began the reckoning, one who owed him ten thousand talents was brought to him; and, as he could not pay, his lord ordered him to be sold, together with his wife and children and all his possessions, and payment to be made. So the slave fell on his knees before him, saying, 'Have patience with me, and I will pay you everything.' And out of pity for him, the lord of that slave released him and forgave him the debt. But that same slave, as he went out, came upon one of his fellow slaves who owed him a hundred denarii; and seizing him by the throat, he said, 'Pay what you owe.' Then his fellow slave fell down and pleaded with him, 'Have patience with me, and I will pay you.' But he refused; then he went and threw him into prison until he would pay the debt. When his fellow slaves saw what had happened, they were greatly distressed, and they went and reported to their lord all that had taken place. Then his lord summoned him and said to him, 'You wicked slave! I forgave you all that debt because you pleaded with me. Should you not have had mercy on your fellow slave, as I had mercy on you?' And in anger his lord handed him over to be tortured until he would pay his entire debt. So my heavenly Father will also do to every one of you, if you do not forgive your brother or sister from your heart."
(Matthew 18:23-35)

QUOTES
ON FORGIVENESS

"I believe forgiveness is the best form of love in any relationship. It takes a strong person to say they're sorry and an even stronger person to forgive."

-Yolanda Hadid

"Forgiveness says you are given another chance to make a new beginning."

-Desmon Tutu

"Forgiveness is not always easy. At times, it feels more painful than the wound we suffered, to forgive the one that inflicted it. And yet there is no peace without forgivness."

-Marianne Williamson

"To forgive is to set a prisoner free and discover that the prisoner was you."

-Lewis B. Smedes

"To err is human; to forgive, divine."

-Alexander Pope

"One forgives to the degree that one loves."

-Francois de La Rochefoucauld

Journal Guide

Please follow these guidelines for each section of the journal

Offender Name
This is the name of the person that caused the hurt that you experienced.

The Offense
This is a general description of the event that caused the hurt.

"I Need Faith to Believe"
In this section, state the spiritual or emotional outcome that God desires your life to reflect AFTER forgiveness.

Exactly what hurt me?
Specify what the offense communicated to you about yourself or how it made you feel.

Statement of Hurt
Use this section to honestly express how much the offense hurt you.

Prayer of Grace
Simply pray this prayer before beginning the next section(s).

Declaration of Release
Write a personal statement to the offender releasing him or her from the offense.

Heavenly Record Removal
Pray this prayer concerning the removal of the eternal record of the offense

Prayer of Blessing
Pray this prayer over the person's life.

Offender Name: _____

The Offense:

_____

_____

_____

"I Need the Faith to Believe"

_____

_____

_____

_____

Exactly what hurt me?

_____

_____

_____

_____

Statement of Hurt:

_____

_____

_____

_____

Prayer for Grace

"Lord, give me the grace to release this offense from my heart. I need your strength to help me do this. In Jesus' name I ask it, AMEN."

Declaration of Release

_____

_____

_____

Heavenly Record Removal

"Father, I ask that you would remove any offense done by (person's name). Please remove it from your heavenly record and let there be no heavenly retribution for what was done to me."

Prayer of Blessing

"Father, I now ask that you will bless (person's name). Bless every area of his/her life and bless the work of his/her hands that they may experience your prosperity and favor. Let his/her life not reflect in any way the offense that was done, but allow it to fully reflect Your love towards him/her."

Date of Forgiveness: *Time :*

Date of Forgiveness: *Time :*

Date of Forgiveness: *Time :*

Offender Name: _____

The Offense:

_____
_____
_____

"I Need the Faith to Believe"

_____
_____
_____
_____

Exactly what hurt me?

_____
_____
_____
_____

Statement of Hurt:

_____
_____
_____
_____

Prayer for Grace

"Lord, give me the grace to release this offense from my heart. I need your strength to help me do this. In Jesus' name I ask it, AMEN."

Declaration of Release

_____

_____

_____

Heavenly Record Removal

"Father, I ask that you would remove any offense done by (person's name). Please remove it from your heavenly record and let there be no heavenly retribution for what was done to me."

Prayer of Blessing

"Father, I now ask that you will bless (person's name). Bless every area of his/her life and bless the work of his/her hands that they may experience your prosperity and favor. Let his/her life not reflect in any way the offense that was done, but allow it to fully reflect Your love towards him/her."

Date of Forgiveness: *Time :*

Date of Forgiveness: *Time :*

Date of Forgiveness: *Time :*

Offender Name: _____

The Offense:

_____
_____
_____

"I Need the Faith to Believe"

_____
_____
_____
_____

Exactly what hurt me?

_____
_____
_____
_____

Statement of Hurt:

_____
_____
_____
_____

Prayer for Grace

"Lord, give me the grace to release this offense from my heart. I need your strength to help me do this. In Jesus' name I ask it, AMEN."

Declaration of Release

_____

_____

_____

Heavenly Record Removal

"Father, I ask that you would remove any offense done by (person's name). Please remove it from your heavenly record and let there be no heavenly retribution for what was done to me."

Prayer of Blessing

"Father, I now ask that you will bless (person's name). Bless every area of his/her life and bless the work of his/her hands that they may experience your prosperity and favor. Let his/her life not reflect in any way the offense that was done, but allow it to fully reflect Your love towards him/her."

Date of Forgiveness: *Time :*

Date of Forgiveness: *Time :*

Date of Forgiveness: *Time :*

Offender Name: _____

The Offense:

_____

_____

_____

"I Need the Faith to Believe"

_____

_____

_____

_____

Exactly what hurt me?

_____

_____

_____

_____

Statement of Hurt:

_____

_____

_____

_____

Prayer for Grace

"Lord, give me the grace to release this offense from my heart. I need your strength to help me do this. In Jesus' name I ask it, AMEN."

Declaration of Release

_____

_____

_____

Heavenly Record Removal

"Father, I ask that you would remove any offense done by (person's name). Please remove it from your heavenly record and let there be no heavenly retribution for what was done to me."

Prayer of Blessing

"Father, I now ask that you will bless (person's name). Bless every area of his/her life and bless the work of his/her hands that they may experience your prosperity and favor. Let his/her life not reflect in any way the offense that was done, but allow it to fully reflect Your love towards him/her."

Date of Forgiveness: *Time :*

Date of Forgiveness: *Time :*

Date of Forgiveness: *Time :*

Offender Name: _____

The Offense:

_____

_____

_____

"I Need the Faith to Believe"

_____

_____

_____

_____

Exactly what hurt me?

_____

_____

_____

_____

Statement of Hurt:

_____

_____

_____

_____

Prayer for Grace

"Lord, give me the grace to release this offense from my heart. I need your strength to help me do this. In Jesus' name I ask it, AMEN."

Declaration of Release

_____

_____

_____

Heavenly Record Removal

"Father, I ask that you would remove any offense done by (person's name). Please remove it from your heavenly record and let there be no heavenly retribution for what was done to me."

Prayer of Blessing

"Father, I now ask that you will bless (person's name). Bless every area of his/her life and bless the work of his/her hands that they may experience your prosperity and favor. Let his/her life not reflect in any way the offense that was done, but allow it to fully reflect Your love towards him/her."

Date of Forgiveness: *Time :*

Date of Forgiveness: *Time :*

Date of Forgiveness: *Time :*

Offender Name: _____

The Offense:

_____
_____
_____

"I Need the Faith to Believe"

_____
_____
_____
_____

Exactly what hurt me?

_____
_____
_____
_____

Statement of Hurt:

_____
_____
_____
_____

Prayer for Grace

"Lord, give me the grace to release this offense from my heart. I need your strength to help me do this. In Jesus' name I ask it, AMEN."

Declaration of Release

_____

_____

_____

Heavenly Record Removal

"Father, I ask that you would remove any offense done by (person's name). Please remove it from your heavenly record and let there be no heavenly retribution for what was done to me."

Prayer of Blessing

"Father, I now ask that you will bless (person's name). Bless every area of his/her life and bless the work of his/her hands that they may experience your prosperity and favor. Let his/her life not reflect in any way the offense that was done, but allow it to fully reflect Your love towards him/her."

Date of Forgiveness: *Time :*

Date of Forgiveness: *Time :*

Date of Forgiveness: *Time :*

Offender Name: _____

The Offense:

_____
_____
_____

"I Need the Faith to Believe"

_____
_____
_____
_____

Exactly what hurt me?

_____
_____
_____
_____

Statement of Hurt:

_____
_____
_____
_____

Prayer for Grace

"Lord, give me the grace to release this offense from my heart. I need your strength to help me do this. In Jesus' name I ask it, AMEN."

Declaration of Release

_____

_____

_____

Heavenly Record Removal

"Father, I ask that you would remove any offense done by (person's name). Please remove it from your heavenly record and let there be no heavenly retribution for what was done to me."

Prayer of Blessing

"Father, I now ask that you will bless (person's name). Bless every area of his/her life and bless the work of his/her hands that they may experience your prosperity and favor. Let his/her life not reflect in any way the offense that was done, but allow it to fully reflect Your love towards him/her."

Date of Forgiveness: *Time :*

Date of Forgiveness: *Time :*

Date of Forgiveness: *Time :*

Offender Name: _____

The Offense:

_____

_____

_____

"I Need the Faith to Believe"

_____

_____

_____

_____

Exactly what hurt me?

_____

_____

_____

_____

Statement of Hurt:

_____

_____

_____

_____

Prayer for Grace

"Lord, give me the grace to release this offense from my heart. I need your strength to help me do this. In Jesus' name I ask it, AMEN."

Declaration of Release

_____

_____

_____

Heavenly Record Removal

"Father, I ask that you would remove any offense done by (person's name). Please remove it from your heavenly record and let there be no heavenly retribution for what was done to me."

Prayer of Blessing

"Father, I now ask that you will bless (person's name). Bless every area of his/her life and bless the work of his/her hands that they may experience your prosperity and favor. Let his/her life not reflect in any way the offense that was done, but allow it to fully reflect Your love towards him/her."

Date of Forgiveness: *Time :*

Date of Forgiveness: *Time :*

Date of Forgiveness: *Time :*

Offender Name: _____

The Offense:

_____

_____

_____

"I Need the Faith to Believe"

_____

_____

_____

_____

Exactly what hurt me?

_____

_____

_____

_____

Statement of Hurt:

_____

_____

_____

_____

Prayer for Grace

"Lord, give me the grace to release this offense from my heart. I need your strength to help me do this. In Jesus' name I ask it, AMEN."

Declaration of Release

_____

_____

_____

Heavenly Record Removal

"Father, I ask that you would remove any offense done by (person's name). Please remove it from your heavenly record and let there be no heavenly retribution for what was done to me."

Prayer of Blessing

"Father, I now ask that you will bless (person's name). Bless every area of his/her life and bless the work of his/her hands that they may experience your prosperity and favor. Let his/her life not reflect in any way the offense that was done, but allow it to fully reflect Your love towards him/her."

Date of Forgiveness: *Time :*

Date of Forgiveness: *Time :*

Date of Forgiveness: *Time :*

Offender Name: _____

The Offense:

_____

_____

_____

"I Need the Faith to Believe"

_____

_____

_____

_____

Exactly what hurt me?

_____

_____

_____

_____

Statement of Hurt:

_____

_____

_____

_____

Prayer for Grace

"Lord, give me the grace to release this offense from my heart. I need your strength to help me do this. In Jesus' name I ask it, AMEN."

Declaration of Release

_____

_____

_____

Heavenly Record Removal

"Father, I ask that you would remove any offense done by (person's name). Please remove it from your heavenly record and let there be no heavenly retribution for what was done to me."

Prayer of Blessing

"Father, I now ask that you will bless (person's name). Bless every area of his/her life and bless the work of his/her hands that they may experience your prosperity and favor. Let his/her life not reflect in any way the offense that was done, but allow it to fully reflect Your love towards him/her."

Date of Forgiveness: *Time :*

Date of Forgiveness: *Time :*

Date of Forgiveness: *Time :*

Offender Name: _____

The Offense:

_____

_____

_____

"I Need the Faith to Believe"

_____

_____

_____

_____

Exactly what hurt me?

_____

_____

_____

_____

Statement of Hurt:

_____

_____

_____

_____

Prayer for Grace

"Lord, give me the grace to release this offense from my heart. I need your strength to help me do this. In Jesus' name I ask it, AMEN."

Declaration of Release

_____

_____

_____

Heavenly Record Removal

"Father, I ask that you would remove any offense done by (person's name). Please remove it from your heavenly record and let there be no heavenly retribution for what was done to me."

Prayer of Blessing

"Father, I now ask that you will bless (person's name). Bless every area of his/her life and bless the work of his/her hands that they may experience your prosperity and favor. Let his/her life not reflect in any way the offense that was done, but allow it to fully reflect Your love towards him/her."

Date of Forgiveness: *Time :*

Date of Forgiveness: *Time :*

Date of Forgiveness: *Time :*

Offender Name: _____

The Offense:

_____

_____

_____

"I Need the Faith to Believe"

_____

_____

_____

_____

Exactly what hurt me?

_____

_____

_____

_____

Statement of Hurt:

_____

_____

_____

_____

Prayer for Grace

"Lord, give me the grace to release this offense from my heart. I need your strength to help me do this. In Jesus' name I ask it, AMEN."

Declaration of Release

_____

_____

_____

Heavenly Record Removal

"Father, I ask that you would remove any offense done by (person's name). Please remove it from your heavenly record and let there be no heavenly retribution for what was done to me."

Prayer of Blessing

"Father, I now ask that you will bless (person's name). Bless every area of his/her life and bless the work of his/her hands that they may experience your prosperity and favor. Let his/her life not reflect in any way the offense that was done, but allow it to fully reflect Your love towards him/her."

Date of Forgiveness:　　　　*Time :*

Date of Forgiveness:　　　　*Time :*

Date of Forgiveness:　　　　*Time :*

Offender Name: _____

The Offense:

_____

_____

_____

"I Need the Faith to Believe"

_____

_____

_____

_____

Exactly what hurt me?

_____

_____

_____

_____

Statement of Hurt:

_____

_____

_____

_____

Prayer for Grace

"Lord, give me the grace to release this offense from my heart. I need your strength to help me do this. In Jesus' name I ask it, AMEN."

Declaration of Release

_____

_____

_____

Heavenly Record Removal

"Father, I ask that you would remove any offense done by (person's name). Please remove it from your heavenly record and let there be no heavenly retribution for what was done to me."

Prayer of Blessing

"Father, I now ask that you will bless (person's name). Bless every area of his/her life and bless the work of his/her hands that they may experience your prosperity and favor. Let his/her life not reflect in any way the offense that was done, but allow it to fully reflect Your love towards him/her."

Date of Forgiveness: *Time :*

Date of Forgiveness: *Time :*

Date of Forgiveness: *Time :*

Offender Name: _____

The Offense:

_____

_____

_____

"I Need the Faith to Believe"

_____

_____

_____

_____

Exactly what hurt me?

_____

_____

_____

_____

Statement of Hurt:

_____

_____

_____

_____

Prayer for Grace

"Lord, give me the grace to release this offense from my heart. I need your strength to help me do this. In Jesus' name I ask it, AMEN."

Declaration of Release

_____

_____

_____

Heavenly Record Removal

"Father, I ask that you would remove any offense done by (person's name). Please remove it from your heavenly record and let there be no heavenly retribution for what was done to me."

Prayer of Blessing

"Father, I now ask that you will bless (person's name). Bless every area of his/her life and bless the work of his/her hands that they may experience your prosperity and favor. Let his/her life not reflect in any way the offense that was done, but allow it to fully reflect Your love towards him/her."

Date of Forgiveness: *Time :*

Date of Forgiveness: *Time :*

Date of Forgiveness: *Time :*

Offender Name: _____

The Offense:

_____
_____
_____

"I Need the Faith to Believe"

_____
_____
_____
_____

Exactly what hurt me?

_____
_____
_____
_____

Statement of Hurt:

_____
_____
_____
_____

Prayer for Grace

"Lord, give me the grace to release this offense from my heart. I need your strength to help me do this. In Jesus' name I ask it, AMEN."

Declaration of Release

_____

_____

_____

Heavenly Record Removal

"Father, I ask that you would remove any offense done by (person's name). Please remove it from your heavenly record and let there be no heavenly retribution for what was done to me."

Prayer of Blessing

"Father, I now ask that you will bless (person's name). Bless every area of his/her life and bless the work of his/her hands that they may experience your prosperity and favor. Let his/her life not reflect in any way the offense that was done, but allow it to fully reflect Your love towards him/her."

Date of Forgiveness: *Time :*

Date of Forgiveness: *Time :*

Date of Forgiveness: *Time :*

NOTES

NOTES

NOTES

NOTES

NOTES

NOTES

NOTES

Made in the USA
Middletown, DE
17 February 2020

84953460R00029